Get Wise

Animals and Us

⇒ do animals have rights?

Jane Bingham

Heinemann
LIBRARY

J179·3

 www.heinemann.co.uk/library
Visit our website to find out more information about **Heinemann Library** books.

To order:
☎ Phone 44 (0) 1865 888066
🖷 Send a fax to 44 (0) 1865 314091
💻 Visit the Heinemann Bookshop at www.heinemann.co.uk/library to browse our catalogue and order online.

First published in Great Britain by Heinemann Library,
Halley Court, Jordan Hill, Oxford OX2 8EJ, part of Harcourt
Education.

Heinemann is a registered trademark of Harcourt
Education Ltd.

Editorial: Lucy Thunder and Harriet Milles
Design: David Poole and Kamae Design
Illustrations: Jeff Anderson
Picture Research: Melissa Allison and Kay Altwegg
Production: Camilla Smith

Originated by Ambassador Litho Ltd
Printed and bound in China, by WKT Company Limited

The paper used to print this book comes from sustainable
resources.

ISBN 0 431 21032 2 (hardback)
09 08 07 06 05
10 9 8 7 6 5 4 3 2 1

ISBN 0 431 21038 1 (paperback)
10 09 08 07 06
10 9 8 7 6 5 4 3 2 1

**British Library Cataloguing in
Publication Data**
Bingham, Jane
(Get Wise). – Animals and Us – do animals have rights?
179.3

A full catalogue record for this book is available from the
British Library.

Acknowledgements
The Publishers would like to thank the following for
permission to reproduce photographs:
pp. **4**, **7** Corbis/Royalty free; p. **5** Camera Press; p. **6**
FLPA/Martin B. Withers; p. **8** Corbis/David Reed; p. **9**
Alamy; p. **10** Ardea London Ltd/John Swedburg; p. **12**
Joe McDonald; p. **13** Harcourt Education/Tudor
Photography; p. **14** Corbis/Jonathan Blair; p. **15** Getty
Images/Photodisc; p. 16 Alamy/imagebroker; p. **18** David
Hoffman Photo Library; p. **19** Alamy/Brand X Pictures;
p. **21** Alamy/Janine Wiedel Photolibrary; pp. 22, 28, 29
RSPCA; p. **23** NHPA/Stephen Dalton; p. **24** Corbis/Carl &
Ann Purcell; p. **25** Alamy/Martin Harvey; p. **26** Alamy/Jeff
Morgan; p. **27** NHPA/James Warwick

Talk time images pp. **7**, **11**, **13**, **19**, **29** Getty
Images/Photodisc

Cover photograph reproduced with permission of PA
Photos/DPA.

The Publishers would like to thank Michaela Miller, former
head of publications at the RSPCA, for her assistance in
the preparation of this book.

Every effort has been made to contact copyright holders
of any material reproduced in this book. Any omissions
will be rectified in subsequent printings if notice is given
to the Publishers.

05JJ3J46

Contents

Words appearing in bold, **like this**, are explained in the Glossary.

How should human beings treat animals?

Humans are ➔ surrounded by other creatures, and we need to treat them well.

Have you ever thought how many animals there are all around us? As well as all the animals we keep as pets, there are wild, farm and working animals. You probably see some of these every day. How do we treat the creatures that share our planet?

Animal needs

All the animals around us have needs – things they have to have in order to survive. Just like human beings, animals need regular food and water, a safe place to sleep and enough space to move around. Without these things they cannot live a happy and healthy life.

In the wild, animals can look after their own needs. But when they are cared for by humans, their owners have a responsibility to make sure all their needs are met.

Animal rights?

Human beings have **rights**. For instance, the right to be free and not owned by anyone else, and the right not to be killed. But should animals have the same rights as humans?

Some **animal rights campaigners** say that animals and humans should have the same rights. However most people believe that animals and humans should be treated differently. They say that humans have a duty to treat animals well, but they do not think that animals should have the same rights as humans.

Exploring animal rights

This book looks at how people and animals live together, and asks questions about the ways that human beings treat their fellow creatures. In the following pages you will find a range of answers to these questions. You will also have the chance to decide what you think.

Unfortunately, some animals do ➲ not live a happy and healthy life. People have to decide whether it is ever right to treat animals like this.

Fact Flash

A dog left unattended in a car on a hot day can die from heat stroke in less than 10 minutes.

Do you have a pet? And, if so, what can you do to make sure it is well and happy? Pets can't complain if they are badly treated so it is up to you to look after them well and make sure that all their needs are met.

Which pet?

Choosing the right pet is an important decision. You and your family need to think hard about whether you can give your pet everything it needs. Is your family out of the house a lot? Do you all hate walking? If so, a dog is not the pet for you. It is unfair to expect a dog to spend long stretches of time alone – and dogs need to be walked every day.

Pet care

In order to stay healthy, pets need regular food and water, plenty of exercise, and a clean, safe **environment**. If your pet lives in a cage or a tank, its home will need regular cleaning. If your pet is ill, you also have a responsibility to take it to the vet.

Having a pet is a big responsibility. Your pet deserves proper care.

Having fun

As well as looking after your pet, you need to spend some time with it. Most animals enjoy attention and companionship. But remember to watch your pet carefully to find out what makes it happy, and never play roughly with it.

 Most pets will love to have fun with you. But only play the sort of games your pet enjoys.

Talk time

What do you do to care for your pet?

Rick: I take my dog for a walk every day – even when it's raining.

Scott: I check the temperature in my fish tank night and morning.

Tanvi: I clean out my hamster's cage once a week.

Lei-Lei: I clean out my rabbits' home too. And when I've finished, I always play with them.

Carelessness costs lives

If pets are not fed regularly or are kept in cramped and unhealthy conditions they can become ill and even die. It is against the **law** to treat animals badly. People who are guilty of cruelty to animals may have to pay a **fine**, and can even be sent to prison.

THINK IT THROUGH

Can anyone look after a pet?

Yes. It is not difficult to remember what an animal needs.

No. Keeping a pet can be hard work. Not everyone makes a good pet owner.

What do YOU think?

How should farm animals be treated?

Fact Flash

The Farm Animal Welfare Council **campaigns** for five animal freedoms: freedom from thirst, hunger, pain and fear, and freedom of movement.

In today's world, farmers need to produce large amounts of food as cheaply as possible, so that supermarkets will buy it. This means that farmers often have to make some difficult choices about the way they treat animals.

Intensive farming

Some farmers try to produce large amounts of cheap food by keeping lots of animals in a small space. Their feed is given straight to them. This is known as **intensive farming**.

Animals **reared** on intensive farms hardly ever get the chance to behave normally. They have very little exercise and some don't even see daylight. Intensive farming is sometimes described as 'factory farming', because the animals are treated like objects in a factory, rather than living beings.

Battery hens, like ➲ these, are forced to spend all their lives in very small cages.

Many people believe that the eggs produced from free-range chickens, like these, are healthier to eat.

Free-range animals

Another group of farmers give their animals freedom to roam outside and find their own food. This is known as **free-range farming**. Many free-range farmers also make sure that their animals do not eat plants that have been sprayed with chemicals. However, free-range animals cost a lot to keep, so food produced like this is more expensive.

The middle way

Many farmers do not run factory farms or free-range farms. They keep their animals in reasonable conditions and allow them some freedom to exercise. However, these farmers still provide most of the animals' feed.

Newsflash

When farm animals are treated badly, they can sometimes develop serious diseases. In 1986, cows in Britain began dying in large numbers from a new disease called bovine spongiform encephalopathy (BSE). Although sheep had suffered for many years from a similar disease called scrapie, no cows had ever caught scrapie.

Scientists discovered that the cause of BSE was the cows' food. Farmers had started feeding cows with a new food made from sheep's brains, and so the disease of scrapie had been passed on to the cows.

THINK IT THROUGH

Should all farms be free-range?

Yes. It is the only way to produce healthy food and treat animals well.

No. Some people can't afford to buy free-range. They need cheap food.

What do YOU think?

Food for thought

Have you ever thought about where your food comes from? Once people start thinking about the food they eat, some decide that they will only eat animals that have been **reared** in a certain way. Others choose to be **vegetarians**, and do not eat any meat or fish.

Which meat?

Many people are concerned about the treatment of animals on farms. When farmers use **intensive farming** methods, their animals have very little freedom. Some people decide that they do not want to eat animals that have been reared like this. They will only eat meat from animals that have had a reasonably natural life and have not suffered.

People who make these choices eat the meat of animals that have been reared on **free-range farms**. They often also choose to eat free-range and **organic** meat because they believe it is better for their health. But free-range and organic meat is expensive, so not everyone can afford to buy it.

⟡ Fish can also be intensively farmed. These fish are kept in a special area, away from the open river.

Going vegetarian

Some people choose to stop eating meat and fish altogether and become vegetarian. They may be unhappy with the thought of animals suffering, or they may not like the idea of eating animals at all.

It is possible to have a very healthy diet without ever eating meat. Meat and fish contain **protein**, which keeps your body strong and healthy. However, vegetarians can get their protein from other foods, such as milk, cheese, eggs and lentils.

Talk time

What food choices have you made?

 Scott: I'm a vegetarian because I love animals and I don't want them to die because of me.

Tanvi: I'm veggie too. I think farmers would be able to feed far more people if they only grew crops.

 Rick: I like meat, but I think free-range stuff tastes best, so we try to buy it when we can.

Lei-Lei: That's what my family does too. And it's good to know the chickens have had a happy life!

THINK IT THROUGH

Does it matter what you eat?

Yes. You should think about what's happened to your food before it reaches your plate.

No. Food is just fuel to give you energy. Who cares where it comes from?

What do YOU think?

Top thoughts

'Animals are my friends, and I don't eat my friends.'

George Bernard Shaw, 20th century Irish playwright and vegetarian

What kind of lives do working animals lead?

Throughout history, people have relied on working animals to help them survive. Even in the modern world, animals do some very important jobs. However, is it right to expect animals to work for us?

Farming help

In the past, animals helped people in many ways. They carried them around, pulled heavy loads, and worked on farms. Nowadays, in many countries, machines usually do these jobs. However, in some areas of the world people still need working animals to help them with their daily tasks.

◗ In many parts of Asia, bullocks pull carts and plough the land.

Special jobs

Working animals play some important roles in the modern world. Horses and dogs help the police in their work. Guide dogs help blind people to live independent lives, and sheep dogs work on farms. Most owners appreciate the valuable job that their animals do, and keep them healthy and contented.

Enjoying a ride

Some animals are kept just for people to ride. Most people think that if a horse is well treated, it can enjoy the ride too. However, it is very important to make sure that the horse has plenty of rest and good food. Horses also need to be groomed regularly and seen by a vet if they show any signs of illness.

Talk time

Have you ever worked with animals?

 Lei-Lei: I work in a stables at the weekends, and we make sure all the horses are really well cared for.

Tanvi: Yeah, me too. We never ride the horses when they're tired.

 Rick: My grandad keeps carrier pigeons, and sometimes I help him fix the messages on to their legs.

Scott: My mum helps to train guide dogs. We take them everywhere with us so they can get used to people and traffic.

🎧 As well as having a working partnership, guide dogs and their owners often become great friends.

THINK IT THROUGH

Should humans expect animals to work for them?

Yes. Animals can help us a lot, and they can enjoy the work.

No. Animals should be free to do what they like.

What do YOU think?

That's entertainment?

Is it right that animals are used to entertain people?

Some animals perform in circuses or star in films, and sometimes they run races. But should animals have to work so hard, just to keep us amused?

Circuses

In the early 20th century, circus animals were trained to do unnatural things. Tigers leapt through hoops, elephants stood on one leg, and seals balanced balls on their noses. However, since the 1980s, most circus tricks have been performed by humans, not animals.

Some circuses still use animals. The circus trainers say that their animals are healthy – but even the most careful trainer cannot prevent their animals from sometimes injuring themselves. Circus animals can also suffer when they have to travel in cages.

Fact Flash

Due to public concern about the welfare of circus animals, some local authorities in the UK have **banned** animal circuses on council-owned land.

Some people believe ➲ that animals only perform like this because they want to.

⟳ Many people believe that elephants should only be seen in the wild, or in wildlife **documentaries**.

Screen stars

In the past, some films and TV shows included animals performing tricks. Today, animals in films are not usually expected to behave in an unnatural way. However, some people think that films should only ever show animals living natural lives.

Racing ahead

In many countries, horses and greyhounds race around tracks while excited crowds cheer them on. This may seem very thrilling, but racing can be dangerous and racehorses often suffer nasty falls.

THINK IT THROUGH

Is it ever OK to make animals perform?

Yes. Animals can enjoy performing.

No. It is cruel and unnatural to make animals do tricks.

What do YOU think?

Zoos - good or bad?

Are all zoos the same – and are they ever a good thing?

People love to see wild animals – and one way they can do this is to visit a zoo. For hundreds of years, people have collected wild animals and kept them in zoos. But is it ever right for animals that were born free to be forced to live in **captivity**?

Bad zoos, good zoos

In some zoos, animals are kept in small cages without enough room for them to get proper exercise. However, over the last fifty years, many zoos have tried to provide animals with a better living **environment**. Most modern zoos are in the country rather than in towns, so animals have more room to move around.

A chance to learn?

Some people think that zoos are a good idea because they give people a chance to see wild animals and learn about their behaviour. Some even say that city zoos are a good thing, because they allow more people to see the animals. However, others say that people should watch wildlife **documentaries** instead.

Zoos like these give animals a great deal of freedom. But some people argue that it is never right to keep wild animals in captivity.

Born free

People who are against zoos say that animals kept in cages often become ill and depressed. Even if animals seem to be happy in captivity, they are still not living natural lives. They may not be living in a climate that suits them, or they may not be eating ideal food.

Keeping safe

Many zoos aim to protect and **conserve** wild animals that are in danger of dying out. Animals such as tigers and pandas are kept in safe conditions in zoos or **wildlife reserves** and encouraged to breed.

DO NOT FEED THE HUMANS

Aren't those humans weird!

THINK IT THROUGH

Are zoos a good thing?

Yes. They allow people to learn about animals and help to prevent rare **species** from dying out.

No. Wild animals should be left alone to get on with their lives.

What do YOU think?

Testing, testing

Should animals be used to test medicines and cosmetics?

Fact Flash

Several cosmetic companies are against experiments on animals. They label their goods 'not tested on animals'.

S ome scientists use animals to test whether certain products or drugs are safe to use on humans. However, many **animal rights campaigners** are against these tests. But is there sometimes a good reason for tests on animals?

Helping people, saving lives

Scientists use animals such as rats or monkeys to test a wide range of different products. Sometimes they test an animal's **reaction** to a perfume, a soap, or a type of make-up to see if it makes them itch or develop a rash. If the animal is **allergic** to that product, the scientists know that humans would be allergic to it too. Then they tell the manufacturers to change their product.

Other experiments use animals to test medicines and drugs. Animals are treated with a new drug to see if it cures a disease, and to check if it has bad **side-effects**.

Some animal rights ➲ campaigners feel so strongly against experiments on animals that they are prepared to break the law.

Talk time

Should products and drugs be tested on animals?

Lei-Lei: I think make-up should always be tested on people, not animals.

Scott: I agree. I've got a really cute pet rat, so I hate to think of rats in pain.

Rick: But aren't sick people more important than animals?

Tanvi: Yeah, my Auntie's got **multiple sclerosis**, so I want scientists to have the best chance of finding a cure for her.

Tests on animals can help scientists to find the right drugs to fight serious diseases like **cancer**.

Humans or animals first?

A large number of people think that drug experiments on animals should continue. They say that human health should be put before the needs of animals.

However, not all tests on animals are a matter of life and death. Why should animals be used to test make-up? Many of the tests cause a lot of suffering to the animals, who feel pain just like humans.

THINK IT THROUGH

Is it right to make animals suffer so that we can have more comfortable lives?

Yes. We should concentrate on stopping disease and suffering in humans.

No. Animals should never have to suffer for our sake.

What do YOU think?

The thrill of the chase?

Why do people
go hunting –
and is it ever
a good thing?

Humans have hunted animals for food for thousands of years, but nowadays some people like to hunt for sport. People shoot wild animals and birds with guns. Anglers catch fish and, until recently, people were allowed to chase foxes. However, is it right that we should chase and kill animals for sport?

Hunting – a harmless sport?

People who support hunting argue that it has always been part of country life. They also say that it is important to keep down the numbers of wild animals, like deer and foxes, because they are a pest. Foxes often attack ducks, geese and chickens on farms. Deer can damage young trees.

People say that a sport like foxhunting also provides jobs for people in the country, such as looking after the horses and dogs used for hunting.

Top thoughts

'Hunting is not a sport. In a sport, both sides should know that they're in the game.'

Paul Rodriguez, US actor and comedian

And they call this fun?

Needless cruelty?

In a hunt, the fox has to run until it is exhausted and then it is attacked by dogs. People who are against hunting think this is very cruel. They agree that foxes can be a pest, but they say it is much better to shoot foxes than hunt them. They also question whether hunting really is good for the countryside. When hunters race through fields after a fox, they can sometimes damage farmers' crops and hedges.

Taking action

Some people feel so strongly against hunting that they have taken action. These people are called hunt saboteurs. Their actions have included spraying the ground to dull the fox's scent – or laying false trails to send the hunters off in the wrong direction. In 2004, the UK government passed a new **law banning** the hunting of foxes as from February 2005.

People who enjoy hunting **organized** big marches in London and put up posters in favour of continuing the sport.

THINK IT THROUGH

Should people be allowed to hunt foxes for sport?

Yes. Foxes are pests, and need to be controlled.

No. Hunting hurts the animal, and is very cruel.

What do YOU think?

Creatures all around us

What can you do to look after the animals in your local environment?

We are surrounded by wild creatures, but many of them are in danger because of our behaviour. How do humans put animals in danger and what can be done to keep our wildlife safe?

Wildlife under threat

Have you ever thought about the enormous impact humans have on the **environment**? Fumes from cars and factories cause air pollution. Chemicals sprayed on plants can cause damage to the plants, and to the animals that eat them. Human waste and **sewage** pumped into rivers and seas can poison and kill fish and water creatures. And human litter left lying around can put wild animals in danger.

Abandoned rubbish ➲ puts animals in great danger. This swan has built her nest in a death trap.

Setting up a bird table is a good way to help and encourage wildlife.

Local help

One way to make your neighbourhood a safer place for wildlife, is to make sure that animals don't come into contact with dangerous litter (see Top Tips). You could organize a litter patrol with your parents and friends to help clear up your local streets.

Taking care

Everyone can make a difference to their local wildlife. Whenever you go out, be sure to treat all animals with care and consideration. Never chase, hurt or frighten an animal. Do not feed animals unsuitable food and never disturb their homes and nests. Be sure that dogs are kept on a lead when sheep and cattle are around and be aware of the dangers of starting a fire.

TOP TIPS

Just putting rubbish inside a dustbin is not enough. Dustbins often get overturned by dogs and other animals. So follow these three simple rules to help keep animals safe.

◎ Always wrap up broken glass in several layers of newspaper.

◎ Crush any plastic pots with narrow necks – animals can get their heads trapped inside these.

◎ Cut up each ring in a plastic 'six-pack' can holder – these can get tangled around animals' heads and legs.

THINK IT THROUGH

Can I make a difference to local wildlife?

Yes. There are lots of simple things I can do.

No. One person can't make a difference – animals need to look after themselves.

What do YOU think?

Why are some animals in danger – and what can be done about it?

In many parts of the world, wild animals are **endangered**. Some **species**, such as the white rhino and the giant panda, have become so rare that they may even die out completely. Why is this happening, and what can be done about it?

Disappearing homes

Every species of animal has its own **habitat**. However, when that habitat changes or disappears, some of the animals that live in it are in danger of dying out. Tropical rainforests are home to two-thirds of the world's wildlife, but they are shrinking fast. Already half the rainforests have been destroyed and the land cleared for farms and homes.

Other habitats are also under threat. Some forests in northern Europe, Asia and America are being cut down so their wood can be used for furniture and paper. The **coral reefs** of the South Pacific Ocean are being damaged by **sewage** and chemical waste.

Everyone enjoys ⮕ looking at wild animals, but we have a responsibility to make sure their environment is unharmed.

Danger at sea

As the human population increases, more and more fish are being caught in the oceans. Modern fishing ships can now catch hundreds of fish at a time. Sometimes, other sea creatures, such as turtles and dolphins, can get trapped and die in fishing nets.

Taking action

In many parts of the world, people are taking action to save damaged habitats. They are working to conserve forests and plant new trees, and to reduce pollution on the land and in the oceans.

People are also working to help endangered species. **Laws** have been passed to stop the hunting of rare animals, including whales, and many countries have strict fishing rules (see pages 26–27).

(see pages 26–27)

Newsflash

Some animals can be put under threat if a new species arrives in their habitat. The Australian bilby (a wild animal similar to a rabbit) is being driven out of large areas of Australia. When the British first settled in Australia they brought rabbits, who took over the burrows of the native bilbies and competed with them for food. Now the rabbits are so widespread that the bilbies are in danger of dying out.

THINK IT THROUGH

Should we try to stop some species dying out?

Yes. Humans have caused the problems so they should try to solve them.

No. It doesn't matter if a few species die out – there are thousands more.

What do YOU think?

🎧 Bilbies, like this one, are becoming increasingly rare in Australia.

Are there laws to protect animals – and how do organizations work for animals' rights?

Fact Flash

The UK charity, the Cats' Protection League, finds a home for a stray cat every two minutes.

Animals all over the world need to be kept safe. There are **laws** to protect wildlife and to prevent cruelty to animals. But laws on their own aren't enough. There are also many **organizations** and charities that work for animal **welfare**.

It's the law

In most parts of the world, the hunting of rare animals has been **banned** and there are also laws against catching whales and seals. Many countries forbid fishing when the fish are breeding, and some ships have to use nets with large enough holes for baby fish to escape.

In 1981, the UK government passed a law, known as The Wildlife and Countryside Act, to protect all animals living in the wild. People who are caught being cruel to wild animals can be made to pay a large **fine**. There are also laws to prevent people being cruel to pets and working animals.

Some organizations ➲ provide a safe home for badly treated animals, such as this horse.

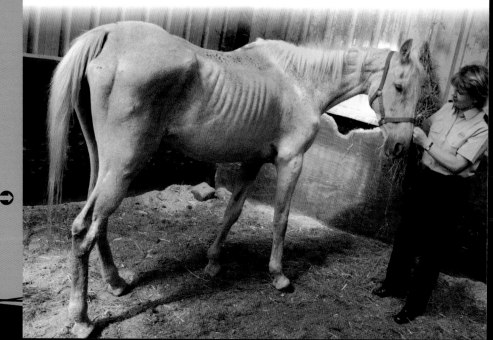

Newsflash

Many animal welfare organizations run public awareness **campaigns**. In 2004, the charity Animals Australia ran a nationwide campaign to stop people sending live farm animals on long journeys overseas. They put up billboards all over the country to make the Australian public more aware of this cruel practice.

This breeding centre in central China works to protect the endangered giant panda.

Working for wider changes

Some animal charities look at the wider picture. The World Wide Fund for Nature (WWF), the International Fund for Animal Welfare and the Born Free Foundation work to protect **endangered species** all over the world. They also aim to educate people about the dangers facing many wild creatures. You can find a short list of organizations and charities that work to protect animals on page 31.

THINK IT THROUGH

Should people give money to animal charities when there are so many poor people who need help?

Yes. Animals have as much right to be helped as people.

No. Poor people's needs should always come first.

What do YOU think?

How can you make a difference to animals' lives?

Everyone can make a difference to animals' lives. You can start by being aware of the wildlife all around you and treating animals with kindness and consideration. However, there are also many other ways to help local animals and wildlife worldwide.

Taking responsibility

Whether you live in the country or the town, there will always be plenty of wildlife around you. And however small they are, all animals need to be treated with respect. Never tease animals or feed them unsuitable food. Never drop litter, and never interfere with a creature's home. If you have a pet, you have a responsibility to provide all its needs and to make sure that it is happy and healthy.

Top thoughts

'When a man has pity on all living creatures, then only is he noble.'

The Buddha, 5th century BCE

Clearing up litter ➲ helps to make the countryside a safer place for animals.

Helping out

There are many positive things you can do to help and encourage local wildlife. You can put food out for birds on a bird table or in a bird feeder – or make a nesting box to encourage birds to nest. With the help of some friends or a teacher, you could start a nature area at home or at school.

Joining in

Often local wildlife groups need **volunteers** to help out by clearing ponds, rivers and paths. This sort of work can be great fun, and you will meet other people who love animals just like you.

Whatever you chose to do, you can make a real difference to the animals that share our planet!

You could help raise ➲ money for your favourite charity, or join in one of their **campaigns**.

Talk time

What do you do to help animals?

Scott: I put out food for the birds. It's great to watch them coming to eat.

Tanvi: I helped clear the rubbish from our local pond. Now it's full of tadpoles!

Rick: I went on a sponsored walk to raise money for **endangered** species.

Lei-Lei: I asked my parents if we could give a home to an abandoned dog.

During the past year we rehomed 69,965 animals

Glossary

allergic if you are allergic to something, it makes you ill

animal rights campaigner someone who believes very strongly in animal rights

ban to make a rule or law to stop something happening

campaign work to make something happen

cancer serious disease in which harmful growths develop in the body

captivity if an animal is in captivity it is not allowed to be free

conserve to protect animals or plants and keep them safe

coral reef large underwater structure made up of the skeletons of millions of sea creatures

documentary film or television programme made about real life

environment natural world of the land, sea and air that surrounds us

endangered in danger of dying out

fine money someone has to pay as a punishment when they have broken a rule or law

free-range farming method of farming where the animals are allowed to roam freely

habitat place where an animal lives naturally

intensive farming method of farming in which lots of animals are kept very close together in pens or cages and fed by the farmer

law rules made by the government of a country which must be obeyed

multiple sclerosis serious disease that stops parts of the body from working properly

organic natural and free from chemicals

organization large group of people all working together to achieve the same aims

protein important part of your diet that keeps you healthy

reaction the way your body acts when it comes into contact with a new substance

rear bring up animals from birth and encourage them to breed

rights something that is fair and that you can expect

sewage liquid and solid waste produced by humans when they go to the toilet

side-effects something that happens after taking a drug, which is not the result that the drug is meant to produce

species group of plants or animals that are alike in most ways

vegetarian someone who does not eat any meat or fish

volunteer someone who offers to do a job without being paid

welfare health, safety and comfort

wildlife reserve large areas of land where animals are protected from harm so that they can live safely

Check it out

Check out these books and websites to find out more about animals' rights and welfare.

Books

Non-fiction

Animal Watch, Roger Few (Dorling Kindersely, 2001)

Wildlife in Danger, Sally Morgan (Franklin Watts, 2000)

Taking Action: WWF, Louise Spilsbury (Heinemann Library, 2001)

Animals Under Threat series (Heinemann Library, 2004)

Fiction

A Zoo in my Luggage, Gerald Durrell (Penguin, 1999)

Animal welfare organizations

Animals Australia: www.animalsaustralia.org

Born Free Foundation: www.bornfree.org.uk

Compassion in World Farming: www.ciwf.org.uk

European Association of Zoos and Aquaria (EAZA): www.eaza.net

Greenpeace (UK): www.greenpeace.org.uk; (Australia): www.greenpeace.org.au

Guide Dogs for the Blind Association: www.gdba.org.uk

RSPCA (UK): www.rspca.org.uk; (Australia): www.rspca.org.au

World Wide Fund for Nature (WWF) (UK): www.wwf-uk.org

(Australia): www.wwf.org.au

Check out the RSPCA's freedom food scheme: www.freedomfood.co.uk